Healthy Eating

by Megan Borgert-Spaniol

BLASTOFF!
2
READERS

BELLWETHER MEDIA • MINNEAPOLIS, MN

AR LG (2.6) 0.5

J
613.2
BORGE

Note to Librarians, Teachers, and Parents:

Blastoff! Readers are carefully developed by literacy experts and combine standards-based content with developmentally appropriate text.

Level 1 provides the most support through repetition of high-frequency words, light text, predictable sentence patterns, and strong visual support.

Level 2 offers early readers a bit more challenge through varied simple sentences, increased text load, and less repetition of high-frequency words.

Level 3 advances early-fluent readers toward fluency through increased text and concept load, less reliance on visuals, longer sentences, and more literary language.

Level 4 builds reading stamina by providing more text per page, increased use of punctuation, greater variation in sentence patterns, and increasingly challenging vocabulary.

Level 5 encourages children to move from "learning to read" to "reading to learn" by providing even more text, varied writing styles, and less familiar topics.

Whichever book is right for your reader, Blastoff! Readers are the perfect books to build confidence and encourage a love of reading that will last a lifetime!

24.00

This edition first published in 2012 by Bellwether Media, Inc.

Library of Congress Cataloging-in-Publication Data
Borgert-Spaniol, Megan, 1989-
  Healthy eating / by Megan Borgert-Spaniol.
    p. cm. – (Blastoff! readers. Eating right with myplate)
  Summary: "Relevant images match informative text in this introduction to healthy eating. Intended for students in kindergarten through third grade"– Provided by publisher.
  Includes bibliographical references and index.
  ISBN 978-1-60014-757-9 (hardcover : alk. paper)
  1. Nutrition–Juvenile literature. 2. Health–Juvenile literature. I. Title.
RA784.B638 2012
613.2–dc23   2011033443

Contents

Healthy Eating with MyPlate

Fruits

Grains

Vegetables

Protein

Dairy

Health

body

grow.

Use **MyPlate** as a mealtime guide. Foods from all five food groups belong on your plate.

5

The Food Groups

Fruits a
canne
full of   min C

This vitamin helps keep your teeth and **gums** healthy. It also helps your body heal.

Protein foods help build
your muscles, bones, skin,
and blood.

12

Meat, **poultry**, and eggs are protein foods. Beans, nuts, and seeds also belong to this group.

Vegetables come in many colors.
Try to eat different colored
vegetables every day.

15

Filling Your Plate

Fruits
fill ha...

Exercising

It is also important to be active for at least one hour each day.

Have a snack before you play.
Drink water when you are thirsty.

Feeling Great

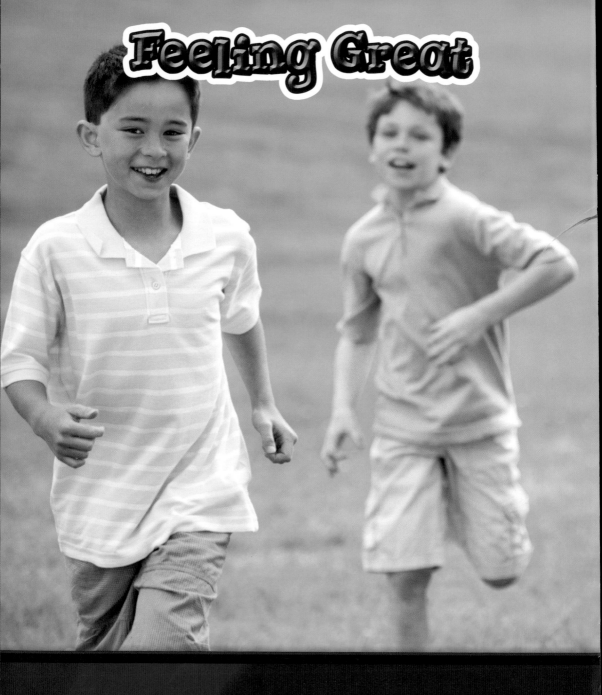

Healthy foods give you energy for work and play.

Glossary

calcium—a part of some foods that your body needs to build strong bones and teeth

fiber—the part of a plant that stays whole as it moves through your body

gums—the soft, pink tissues that hold your teeth in place

MyPlate—a guide that shows the kinds and amounts of food you should eat each day

poultry—the meat of birds that are raised on farms; chicken and turkey are kinds of poultry.

vitamin A—a part of some foods that is good for your eyes and skin

vitamin C—a part of some foods that helps keep your teeth and gums healthy; vitamin C also helps your body heal.

vitamin D—a part of some foods that helps your body use calcium

whole grains—grain foods that are made with the entire grain kernel; whole wheat, brown rice, and oatmeal are whole grains.

To Learn More

AT THE LIBRARY

Miller, Edward. *The Monster Health Book: A Guide to Eating Healthy, Being Active & Feeling Great for Monsters & Kids!* New York, N.Y.: Holiday House, 2006.

Rabe, Tish. *Oh, the Things You Can Do that Are Good for You!* New York, N.Y.: Random House, 2001.

Rockwell, Lizzy. *Good Enough to Eat: A Kid's Guide to Food and Nutrition.* New York, N.Y.: HarperCollins Publishers, 1999.

ON THE WEB

Learning more about healthy eating is as easy as 1, 2, 3.

1. Go to www.factsurfer.com.

2. Enter "healthy eating" into the search box.

3. Click the "Surf" button and you will see a list of related Web sites.

With factsurfer.com, finding more information is just a click away.

Index

The images in this book are reproduced through the courtesy of: Jose Luis Pelaez Inc / Photolibrary, front cover; U.S. Department of Agriculture, Center for Nutrition Policy and Promotion, p. 4; Juan Martinez, pp. 5, 7, 8, 11; 13; 15; Rodolfo Benitez / Getty Images, p. 6; Monkey Business Images, p. 9; Image Source / Getty Images, p. 10; Yuri Arcurs, p. 12; BLOOMimage / Getty Images, p. 14; Monkey Business Images / Photolibrary, pp. 16-17; Imagesource / Photolibrary, pp. 18-19; Christopher Futcher, pp. 20-21.